W9-CMK-076

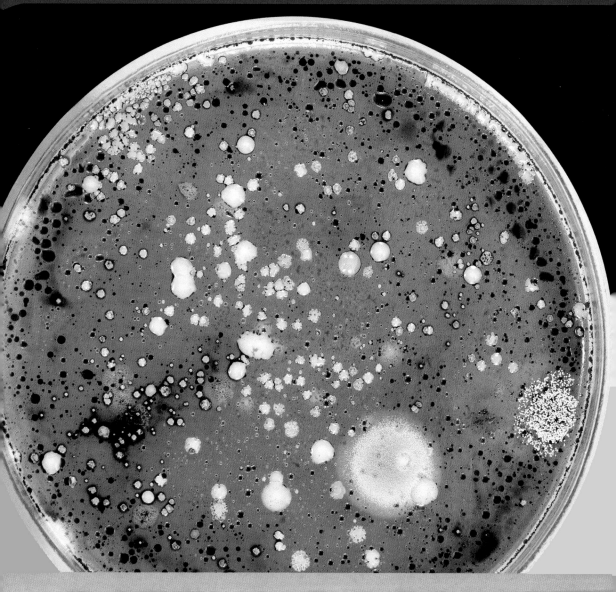

BATTLING AGAINST
DRUG-RESISTANT BACTERIA

by Tammy Gagne

STORY
LIBRARY

www.12StoryLibrary.com

12-Story Library is an imprint of Peterson Publishing Company and Press Room Editions.

Produced for 12-Story Library by Red Line Editorial

Photographs ©: Satirus/Shutterstock Images, cover, 1; kdshutterman/Shutterstock Images, 4; Dusan Petkovic/Shutterstock Images, 5; El Nariz/Shutterstock Images, 6; Zaharia Bogdan Rares/Shutterstock Images, 7; Daniel Jedzura/Shutterstock Images, 8; Tashi-Delek/iStockphoto, 9; Suttha Burawonk/Shutterstock Images, 10; Joe Raedle/Getty Images News/Thinkstock, 11, 25; zmeel/iStockphoto, 13; Everett Historical/Shutterstock Images, 14; TBE/iStockphoto, 15; ktsimage/iStockphoto, 16; Andrey Prokhorov/iStockphoto, 17; bluedog studio/Shutterstock Images, 19, 29; Bhakpong/Shutterstock Images, 20; David Duprey/AP Images, 21; Oxford Science Archive/Heritage Images/Glow Images, 22; Christopher Furlong/Getty Images News/Thinkstock, 24, 28; Sirikornt/iStockphoto, 26; Burlingham/Shutterstock Images, 27

Library of Congress Cataloging-in-Publication Data
Names: Gagne, Tammy, author.
Title: Battling against drug-resistant bacteria / by Tammy Gagne.
Description: North Mankato, MN : 12-Story Library, 2017. | Series: Science
    frontiers | Audience: Grades 4 to 6. | Includes bibliographical
    references and index.
Identifiers: LCCN 2016007567 (print) | LCCN 2016011458 (ebook) | ISBN
    9781632353733 (library bound : alk. paper) | ISBN 9781632353900 (pbk. :
    alk. paper) | ISBN 9781621435143 (hosted ebook)
Subjects: LCSH: Drug resistance in microorganisms--Juvenile literature. |
    Drug resistance--Juvenile literature. | Bacterial diseases--Juvenile
    literature. | Antibiotics--Development--Juvenile literature. | Public
    health--Juvenile literature.
Classification: LCC QR177 .G34 2017 (print) | LCC QR177 (ebook) | DDC
    616.9/201--dc23
LC record available at http://lccn.loc.gov/2016007567

Printed in the United States of America
Mankato, MN
May, 2016

Table of Contents

Many Bacteria Are Becoming Resistant to Antibiotics

Nearly everyone gets an infection at some point in his or her life. People pass bacteria, or germs, to other people every day. Neither the giver nor the receiver has any idea it is happening. Later, the person who picked up the germs gets sick or injured. A bad sore throat or painful cuts that will not heal are both signs of a possible infection. Most of the time medicine from a quick doctor's visit can fix the problem. But sometimes medicine does not kill the bacteria.

Antibiotics are medicines designed to fight bacteria. Over time, some bacteria have become resistant to these medications. This has happened for many reasons. One of the biggest causes is that people are using too many antibiotics. Products made

Most cuts will heal without problems if they are taken care of and cleaned.

Farmers use antibiotics to stop illness from spreading between animals.

to prevent germs from spreading have added to the problem. Antibacterial soaps are supposed to help keep people healthy. But germs have been exposed to these products. Because of this, many bacteria have built up a tolerance for antibiotics.

Overuse of antibiotics is not limited to just humans. Even some of the meat we eat contains antibiotics. Many farmers use these medicines to keep the animals from getting sick. When we eat meat that was raised on antibiotics, we consume small amounts of the medicine too. All of these antibiotics have left sick people in a tough situation. They need medicine to fight off their infections, but many medicines are no longer working.

2 million
Number of US people who become infected with drug-resistant bacteria each year.

- Antibiotics are not killing certain bacteria as they once did.
- Some bacteria have become resistant to drugs because antibiotics are overused.
- Antibacterial soaps have caused some bacteria to build up a tolerance to antibiotics.
- People eat antibiotics in meat without realizing it.

5

Drug Resistance Makes It Harder to Fight Superbugs

Doctors have used antibiotics to fight bacteria for more than 70 years. Yet the fight against germs has become tougher over time. Bacteria have been exposed to antibiotics. They have built up a tolerance to the drugs. Many types of bacteria are now considered superbugs. This means they are much harder to fight than other bacteria.

One of the biggest threats doctors see today is nontyphoidal salmonella. Patients usually get sick from eating food or water with these bacteria in it. Common reactions include stomach pain, fever, and vomiting. Salmonella bacteria have been resistant to several antibiotics for many years now. The bacteria have become resistant to even more drugs recently.

Group A *streptococcus* (GAS) is among the most resistant types of bacteria. GAS causes strep throat. Strep throat begins with a

If not handled or cooked properly, meat can grow salmonella.

KEEPING GERMS FROM SPREADING

Drug-resistant bacteria do not pass from person to person only in a community. They can also spread from one hospital patient to the next. Hospital workers can help prevent this problem by washing their hands thoroughly between patients. Germs can still be passed even if a doctor or nurse does not touch a patient. Bacteria can survive on items such as door handles and call buttons. Equipment can also spread germs.

severe sore throat. It can lead to more serious health problems if not treated. GAS can cause skin infections and even scarlet fever. This serious disease causes a high fever and a red rash.

The most accurate test for strep throat takes several days. Many doctors use a rapid strep test instead. This quicker test allows doctors to prescribe antibiotics right

away. But some patients turn out not to have strep. Using antibiotics when they are not needed makes the drugs less effective over time.

Doctors collect and test bacteria such as GAS on petri dishes.

Researchers Work to Find Solutions to Superbugs

Infectious disease specialists are special doctors. They work to solve the problem of drug resistance. They cannot stop resistance completely though. Bacteria have managed to survive on this planet for millions of years. Germs are so widespread that they cannot be wiped out. Instead, doctors need new ways to treat bacterial illnesses. Some types of bacteria are good and even keep people healthy by fighting off other bad bacteria.

Meningitis is a deadly disease that can be caused by several types of bacteria. The most effective treatment was penicillin. Over time, these bacteria have become resistant to this antibiotic.

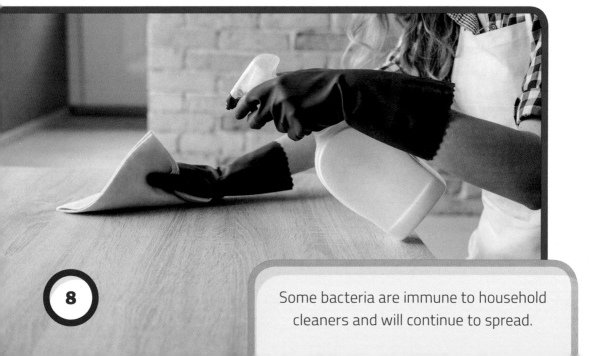

Some bacteria are immune to household cleaners and will continue to spread.

Thankfully, the disease can often be treated successfully with another antibiotic. When one antibiotic does not work, another type may offer a solution.

Many researchers are developing new antibiotics. New drugs have a better chance at curing illness. This is because bacteria have not built up resistance to them yet. But developing new drugs takes a long time. It is also expensive. After a new medication is created, it has to be tested to make sure it is both safe and effective.

Doctors could prescribe fewer antibiotics if they knew which bacteria were present. For this reason some researchers are working to create tests to diagnose viruses.

The process of developing new antibiotics is long and expensive.

95

Percent of experimental medications studied that prove to be neither safe nor effective.

- Infectious disease specialists study drug resistance.
- Drug-resistant bacteria cannot be wiped out completely.
- Doctors need new antibiotics to fight drug-resistant bacteria.
- Developing new antibiotics is expensive and time-consuming.

THINK ABOUT IT

The overuse of antibiotics has made drug-resistant bacteria a bigger problem. Based on what you have read here, how do you think better testing would help reduce antibiotic use?

9

Treatments Are Vital for Patients Fighting Bacteria

The idea of becoming ill from drug-resistant bacteria is scary. Patients are more likely to die from these types of bacteria than from others.

People who do survive are usually sick for long periods of time. Many of them also end up with long-term disabilities. Meningitis, for instance,

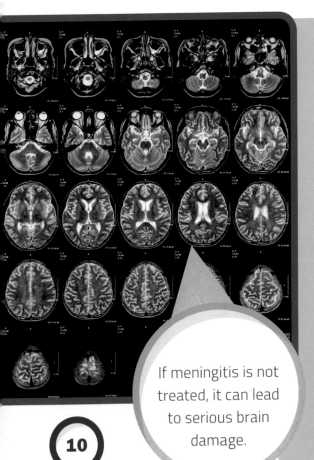

If meningitis is not treated, it can lead to serious brain damage.

MAKING A DIFFICULT FIGHT EVEN TOUGHER

Some diseases are already hard to treat without the added problem of drug resistance. One of those illnesses is tuberculosis. This bacterial disease attacks a person's lungs. Tuberculosis bacteria can also become resistant to antibiotics. Although a tuberculosis vaccine exists, it does not work in many cases. Between eight and nine million people still become infected with tuberculosis each year. Fighting this disease will only become more challenging if a solution to drug resistance is not found soon.

can lead to hearing and vision loss, as well as brain damage.

People who do not receive prompt treatment for bacterial infections may be at the highest risk for death. As they have become stronger, drug-resistant superbugs have gotten better at killing a patient's immune cells. These cells are a person's only way of fighting the bacteria without medication. Meningitis sickens patients quickly. Doctors must act fast to save the lives of patients with this deadly illness.

Some researchers are focused on preventing illnesses instead of treating them. They believe the best defense against drug-resistant bacteria is the development of vaccines. These shots or nasal sprays trigger a person's immune system to fight off bacteria before an illness can develop.

23,000
Number of US patients who die each year after becoming ill from drug-resistant bacteria.

- Superbugs are more likely to kill patients than other types of bacteria are.
- People who do not seek medical treatment quickly face the highest risk of death.
- Drug-resistant bacteria have learned to kill immune cells.
- Vaccines could help prevent illnesses caused by drug-resistant bacteria.

Superbugs Are Deadlier Than Once Believed

Doctors once thought bacteria became weaker as they turned drug resistant. They believed that as bacteria cells stopped taking in antibiotics, they also stopped taking in the nutrients needed to survive. But recent studies have shown this is not the case. Researchers have found that drug-resistant bacteria are actually more powerful, not less, than other types of bacteria.

This new information makes the job of fighting superbugs even harder. Still, scientists are hopeful they can find weaknesses in these germs. One of those weaknesses might be proteins on the outside of bacteria cells. Researchers are trying to develop antibodies that will attack these proteins. If the scientists are successful, doctors might have a new way to kill dangerous bacteria.

The ability to destroy bacteria cells this way could make a big difference in fighting drug-resistant bacteria.

3,000
Number of people who participate in a drug study before a medication becomes available to other patients.

- Doctors once thought bacteria weakened as they became resistant to antibiotics.
- They now know that drug-resistant bacteria are deadlier than other bacteria.
- Scientists may be able to destroy bacteria cells from the outside in.
- Antibodies that destroy proteins could help patients fight off drug-resistant bacteria without antibiotics.

Doctors could give patients who are most at risk vaccines before they become ill. If they come in contact with drug-resistant bacteria, these patients could fight the germs without antibiotics.

Superbugs infect more than two million people nationwide each year.

New Antibiotics Offer Smaller Paydays

Drug resistance is not new. Penicillin, the first antibiotic drug, was discovered in 1928. Doctors began seeing resistance to it within 10 years of the first drug trials. Still, people did not take the problem seriously. Perhaps they assumed that another drug could be found. For many years, the development of new antibiotics was a steady business. This has changed over the last 20 years, however. The number of drug companies making antibiotics dropped from 18 in 1994 to four in 2014. The simple reason is money.

If more antibiotics are created, drug-resistant bacteria could be destroyed. The problem is that most drug companies are not interested in discovering new antibiotics. The cost of creating this type of drug is too high. Companies cannot make back all the money they spend developing these medications.

Most doctors will not prescribe new antibiotics until they have tried all other options. This approach helps

Penicillin was being mass-produced by the 1940s.

A WORLDWIDE PROBLEM

Every country in the world is dealing with the problem of drug-resistant bacteria. Modern transportation makes it an even bigger challenge. People carrying drug-resistant bacteria take it with them whenever they travel. People can also come into contact with drug-resistant bacteria in other countries. The more a country overuses antibiotics, the more likely patients are to pick up a superbug.

$5 million
Cost of creating a new drug.

- Drug resistance is not a new problem.
- Fewer drug companies have developed new antibiotics over the last 20 years.
- Doctors must prescribe fewer unnecessary antibiotics to decrease resistance.
- Developing new antibiotics is not profitable for drug companies.

prevent resistance to the new drugs from overuse. It also means drug companies sell fewer of the new drugs they spent large amounts of money developing. If drug companies do not make enough money from a medication, they will focus on developing drugs they can sell more of instead.

Novartis is one drug company that creates and develops antibiotics.

Doctors Are Seeking Alternative Treatments

Doctors cannot stop drug resistance. Instead, they must change their treatment plans to work around this problem. Researchers across the world are working on drug resistance. Some discoveries have led to creative solutions.

Doctors in Eastern Europe have turned to viruses for help. Researchers have found that viruses called phages are good at eating bacteria. Phages do not harm the patient while they kill the bacteria either. They appear to offer a great alternative to antibiotics. They kill bacteria with no apparent side effects. Still, they have not been tested in the United States for safety and effectiveness.

Another possibility is the use of DNA. Antibiotics kill bacteria by attacking the cells' functions. Researchers at Oregon State University have created special DNA that disrupts bacteria's genes. One might say these scientists are using DNA to

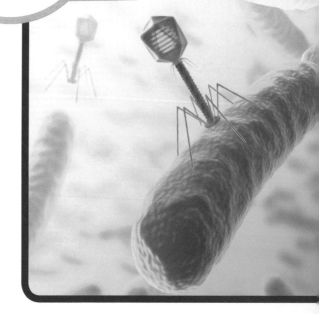

Phages enter the body and destroy bad bacteria.

DNA is a long molecule that holds each person's genetic code.

reprogram the bacteria so they work differently. This approach has not been tested yet for safety.

THINK ABOUT IT

The alternative treatments mentioned here sound like they could solve the problem of resistance. But they cannot be used yet on human patients in the United States. Find one or two sentences in the main text section that explain why this is the case.

10
Number of years before phages might be approved for use in the United States.

- Doctors must find ways to work around the problem of drug resistance.
- Sometimes using a different antibiotic is enough.
- Viruses called phages might become an alternative in treating bacterial infections.
- Eastern European doctors currently use phages.

8

Scientists Find Promising Antibiotic in Dirt

Soil naturally contains many types of bacteria. Studying these bacteria has led to the discovery of numerous antibiotics. These antibiotics grew from the bacteria themselves. In order to develop new antibiotics from soil, scientists must be able to grow the bacteria in their labs. Only one percent of soil bacteria will grow in a laboratory, however. Scientists have not been able to study the other 99 percent of soil bacteria. This is another reason so few antibiotics have been developed in recent years. While scientists have a good idea of where to find the bacteria they need, they cannot get it to grow where they need it.

A team at Northeastern University in Boston, Massachusetts, may have solved this problem. They found a way to study soil bacteria without moving it to a lab. The team uses a device that traps cells but allows natural nutrients into a soil sample. This allows the bacteria to survive.

The team has already developed a new antibiotic. Tests have

A LITTLE MORE TIME

A new antibiotic cannot solve the problem of drug resistance by itself. Over time, bacteria will likely become resistant to a newer antibiotic as well. New antibiotics give researchers several more years to come up with other treatment options though. The less people depend on a new drug, the more time doctors have to find alternatives.

Researchers are hoping soil will provide the answer to new antibiotics.

10,000
Number of bacteria strains the Northeastern University team has tested so far against their new antibiotic.

- Studying soil samples has led to new antibiotic discoveries.
- Most bacteria found in soil will not grow in a lab.
- Northeastern University found a way around this problem.
- The team discovered an antibiotic that can kill drug-resistant bacteria.

shown that this antibiotic can kill a wide range of bacteria. It has even destroyed bacteria that have shown resistance to other drugs. More testing is needed before this antibiotic could be available for use in human patients. But it could make a big difference. Other new antibiotics could also be developed from studying soil.

A Smart Bandage Could Help Lessen Antibiotic Use

Until better options are available, doctors are still prescribing antibiotics when needed. Doctors can keep resistance low by avoiding these drugs whenever possible. It is important to know when an antibiotic treatment is needed right away. Prompt treatment often offers the best results.

When people with burns visit the doctor, many are treated with antibiotics. This is a safety measure. Even doctors do not know if an infection will occur. One study showed that only seven percent of burn patients actually develop infections, but 25 percent are treated with antibiotics.

It is important for burns to be treated with antibiotics and then covered to avoid infection.

The University of Bath in England has come up with a way to avoid unneeded antibiotics for burns. Researchers at the school created a special bandage. It turns bright green before the person wearing it is about to develop an infection. This device is still being tested. It is not yet available to doctors.

The bandage sensor detects certain bacteria in wounds.

- Even as doctors try to prescribe fewer antibiotics, some people truly need them.
- It can be difficult to know when an infection will occur.
- Fast treatment can keep a minor infection from becoming a more serious one.
- Researchers have developed a new bandage that knows when an infection is starting.

Saliva May Offer a Solution

Some scientists are looking inside the human body for a solution to drug-resistant bacteria. Saliva, tears, and other bodily fluids contain proteins called lytic enzymes. These proteins can kill bacteria.

Alexander Fleming won the Nobel Prize in 1945 for his work and research.

NOT A CURE-ALL

When many people get sick, they think they need antibiotics. Some patients even ask their doctors for these drugs. But antibiotics will not help in many situations. Viruses cause more than half of sore throats. They will not get better any faster with antibiotic treatment. Many ear infections are the same way. Doctors estimate that 95 percent of bronchitis cases are viral. Still, some doctors write prescriptions. People believe they are getting better because of the drugs. But it is actually their body healing naturally.

10

Approximate number of years infectious disease specialists spend going to school and training.

- Proteins called lytic enzymes can kill bacteria.
- Alexander Fleming studied these proteins before he discovered penicillin.
- Today, scientists are looking to lytic enzymes as a way to fight bacteria.
- Additional study could lead to a way to treat bacterial illnesses without antibiotics.

The idea that these proteins could be used to fight bacteria is not new. Alexander Fleming, a biologist, began studying these proteins in 1923. It was not until 1928 that he discovered the first antibiotic, penicillin. His success with penicillin left this other idea largely unexplored—until recently.

Scientists today are testing different types of lytic enzymes to see how quickly and effectively they can kill bacteria. Each type kills a specific bacteria. If these proteins can destroy drug-resistant bacteria, they could become the answer to fighting bacterial illnesses without the use of antibiotics.

Developers Add Decoys to the Drugs

New antibiotics and different treatments are two approaches to the drug resistance problem. A combination of these methods may be most effective. Some scientists are working to change existing antibiotics to make them more effective.

This idea involves adding special molecules to antibiotics. The bacteria mistake these decoy molecules for parts of the medicine even though they are not. Researchers have added a decoy molecule to penicillin for this purpose. It tricks the bacteria into thinking it is part of the original drug. The bacteria respond by attacking the decoy instead of the antibiotic itself.

This approach might be a temporary solution. It could buy important time, however. Even after new antibiotics are discovered,

Future researchers must find new ways to treat drug-resistant bacteria.

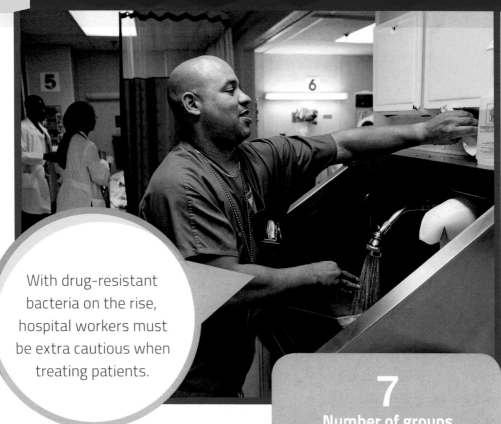

With drug-resistant bacteria on the rise, hospital workers must be extra cautious when treating patients.

a treatment like this could make it less necessary to use a new drug. As long as decoys work, doctors could save new antibiotics for when they are necessary.

THINK ABOUT IT

Many drugs have side effects. Do you think adding decoy molecules to an antibiotic could add side effects to the medication? How would researchers know if this was the case?

7
Number of groups of antibiotics available today.

- Developing new antibiotics and other treatments are not the only options for dealing with drug resistance.
- Antibiotics can be altered to include decoy molecules.
- Bacteria attack the decoys instead of the antibiotic.
- This solution could buy more time for researchers to discover new antibiotics.

Patients Protect Themselves from Superbugs

It is important to understand that not all bacteria are bad. Some germs inside the human body help people fight infections. Also, not all antibiotics are the same. Some are much stronger than others. These more powerful drugs can kill off good bacteria along with an infection. Doctors have learned they should only use the strongest antibiotics for the worst situations.

One type of bad bacteria is called *Clostridium difficile* (C. diff). This bacteria is often found in hospitals. It has also been linked to doctors' and dentists' offices. For this reason, it is smart to wash your hands after spending time in any medical building.

Even modern medicine is not an exact science. Doctors often have to try different treatments before they find one that works for a patient.

Washing your hands for two minutes after being in public will get rid of many germs.

Misusing antibiotics can lead to other health problems.

The best way to help them accomplish this goal is to listen carefully and follow instructions when taking antibiotics. There is also nothing wrong with asking if an antibiotic is necessary.

1,000
Number of different bacteria inside a human's digestive tract.

- Some types of good bacteria help people fight infections.
- Some antibiotics can kill good bacteria along with the bad ones.
- Researchers think some antibiotics may cause an increased risk of infection.
- Handwashing is important to avoid infection.

ANTIBIOTICS IN MEAT

Approximately 80 percent of the antibiotics used in the United States go to farm animals. This practice began with good intentions. If an animal has an infection, people could get sick from eating the meat. The problem is that many farmers now use antibiotics on healthy animals to prevent illness. Anyone who eats non-organic meat may also be consuming antibiotics. This can lower their ability to fight drug-resistant bacteria.

Fact Sheet

- Antibacterial soaps and hand gels are made to prevent the spread of germs. You may see these products when you visit a doctor's office or hospital. Before using any hand cleaner, check the label. Avoid products made with an ingredient called triclosan, as these products may add to the problem of drug-resistant bacteria.

- Some patients ask for antibiotics on their first trip to the doctor to prevent the need for a second visit. They then take the medicine before they know they indeed have a bacterial infection. Doctors can cut down on this practice by calling in a prescription only when they know it is the best treatment.

- Vaccines offer a possible solution to antibiotic resistance. Unfortunately, some people cannot receive vaccines because they are allergic to one or more ingredients. These patients often need the most powerful antibiotics, but taking them for long periods of time only increases their chances of developing a resistance problem.

- Drug companies make most of their money from drugs that people take on a regular basis. Since patients should not take antibiotics any longer than necessary, this is another reason that drug companies have lost interest in making antibiotics. This too is one of the greatest obstacles in the fight against drug-resistant bacteria.

- Doctors have known about drug resistance since shortly after penicillin was introduced. Resistance has existed long before this, however. Bacteria have lived on the planet for millions—perhaps even billions—of years. During this time they have fought off many natural substances that have threatened their existence. No matter how many antibiotics are created, bacteria will continue to survive.

- Education is one of our best tools in the fight against drug-resistant bacteria. As more people learn about the problem, they can adjust their habits to reduce their risk for infections. Simply cleaning a cut and placing a bandage on it instead of applying antibiotic ointment can make a difference.

Glossary

antibodies
Substances produced by special cells of the body to fight illness.

disabilities
Illnesses or injuries that limit a person's abilities, both mental and physical.

molecule
The smallest particle of a substance having all the characteristics of the substance.

prescribe
To order or direct the use of something as a remedy.

profitable
Producing a financial gain.

proteins
Any of numerous substances that consist of chains of amino acids.

resistant
Showing the ability to fight against something.

side effects
Often harmful and unwanted results that occur along with the basic desired results.

tolerance
The ability to adjust to a drug so that its effects are experienced less strongly.

vaccine
A substance that is injected into a person to protect against a specific disease.

For More Information

Books

Klosterman, Lorrie. *Drug-Resistant Superbugs*. Tarrytown, NY: Marshall Cavendish, 2010.

Williams, Mary E. *Antibiotics*. Detroit: Greenhaven, 2014.

Wilsdon, Christina. *Ultimate Bodypedia: An Amazing Inside-Out Tour of the Human Body*. Washington, DC: National Geographic, 2014.

Visit 12StoryLibrary.com

Scan the code or use your school's login at **12StoryLibrary.com** for recent updates about this topic and a full digital version of this book. Enjoy free access to:

- Digital ebook
- Breaking news updates
- Live content feeds
- Videos, interactive maps, and graphics
- Additional web resources

Note to educators: Visit 12StoryLibrary.com/register to sign up for free premium website access. Enjoy live content plus a full digital version of every 12-Story Library book you own for every student at your school.

Index

antibiotics, 4–5, 6–7, 9, 10, 12–13, 14, 15, 16, 18–19, 20–21, 23, 24–25, 26–27

bandage, 21
bronchitis, 23
burn patients, 20–21

Clostridium difficile (C. diff), 26

decoy molecules, 24–25
doctors, 4, 6–7, 8–9, 11, 12–13, 14, 16, 18, 20–21, 23, 25, 26
drug companies, 14–15

England, 21

farmers, 5, 27
Fleming, Alexander, 23

germs, 4–5, 6, 7, 8, 12–13, 26
group A *streptococcus* (GAS), 6–7

immune cells, 11
infections, 4–5, 7, 11, 20–21, 23, 26, 27
infectious disease specialists, 8

lytic enzymes, 22–23

medicines, 4–5, 24, 26
meningitis, 8, 11

Northeastern University, 18

Oregon State University, 16

penicillin, 8, 14, 23, 24
phages, 16

prescriptions, 23
proteins, 12, 22–23

salmonella, 6
soil, 18–19
strep throat, 6–7
superbugs, 6, 8, 11, 12, 15, 26

tolerance, 5, 6
transportation, 15
treatments, 8, 11, 16, 17, 18, 20, 23, 24–25, 26
tuberculosis, 10

United States, 16, 17, 27
University of Bath, 21

vaccines, 10, 11, 13
viruses, 9, 16, 23

About the Author

Tammy Gagne has written more than 150 books for adults and children. She resides in northern New England with her husband and son. One of her favorite pastimes is visiting schools to talk to kids about the writing process.